Ringers

BILL GREENWELL

Published by Cinnamon Press
Meirion House
Glan yr afon
Tanygrisiau
Blaenau Ffestiniog
Gwynedd
LL41 3SU
www.cinnamonpress.com

The right of Bill Greenwell to be identified as author of this work
has been asserted by him in accordance with the Copyright,
Designs and Patent Act, 1988. Copyright © 2011 Bill Greenwell
ISBN: 978-1-907090-47-9

British Library Cataloguing in Publication Data. A CIP record for
this book can be obtained from the British Library.

Designed and typeset in Palatino by Cinnamon Press.
Cover from original artwork © 'Fresh Fish on Ice at Market' by
Darryl Brooks, agency: dreamstime
Cover design by Jan Fortune

Printed in Poland

Cinnamon Press is represented in the UK by Inpress Ltd
www.inpressbooks.co.uk and in Wales by the Welsh Books
Council www.cllc.org.uk.

Acknowledgements

I'd like to thank all of the following who've helped shape this collection: Jane Draycott, Julie-ann Rowell, Basil Ransome-Davies, Boyd Tonkin, Graham Mort, Melissa Bailey, Virginia Astley, Jan Fortune; Linda Anderson, Derek Neale; John Corless, Debbie Samson, Annia Lekka, Laila Farnes, Christina Lloyd, Rosalind Stopps; everyone at Poetry Clinic and Poetry Pond; and Rachel McGovern.

Some of the poems included here (or versions of them) have been published previously in either printed or electronic format, in *Smiths Knoll*, *The Rialto*, *The Spectator*, *The Literary Review*, *Orbis*, *Envoi*, *The Independent* (which commissioned the Blake and Auden parodies), *Chimaera*, *Anon*, *Lightenuponline*, *Iota*, *Shit Creek Review*, *Staple*, and www.theweeklypoem.com; or have won prizes in the Kent & Sussex, Wigtown, Troubadour or Yeovil poetry competitions. The author gratefully acknowledges the support of these publications and their editors.

Contents

to Morgaine

Ringers

Keys

Sometimes you come across a bunch, fob-happy,
just hanging, like a dead pendulum. And vaguely,
they take you to doors and cabinets, to parked cars,
in houses and on streets you don't inhabit.

It's always early autumn with keys. They wait
impassively, slowly rusting, all their desires
lost in distant locks. They have quite forgotten
the scramble of your hands, the way they hunched

in your pocket, or under the dashboard, hiding
while you pasted your face with panic. You were
in love with them, then. They let you in.
You touched them unconsciously, ran your dabs

along their lengths, their bulleted grooves,
their edges rising and falling like the last heartbeats
on a hospital monitor. You knew them in the dark,
lavished their barrels. And now you can't recall

which homes they opened, which secret places
they gave you, and why they were so important.
You held them. They welcomed you, somewhere,
blind with desire. They touch you, uncertain.

Bells

The bell goes. Your mother, slake-naked, runs
for her hasty clothes, all smiles and wonder.
Of course this is romantic. But usually the alarm
is beaten to it, usually she shifts its large lever
off, before it rattles her lids. Not today.

He has been watching the bakelite phone for several
minutes, when, bring-bring, the bell goes.
The gynaecologist has ripped you, in a sweat
of mucus and madder, into existence:
right on cue, it's you, the little caesar.

You're thinking ink, worms, milk, puddle,
when the bell goes. The corridors run forwards
and drag you sideways. Your feet are scuffed,
your laces trail. Under embarrassed Africa, you
sit in rows, thinking at regular intervals.

You bend over the engines, when the bell
goes off. Your head's a hammer. You punch the clock,
and are swept to the yawning gates.
You come home with a hob-nailed face,
and lie on the bed like emptied clothes.

Inside your clenched head, the bell goes off
with dim abandon. She strokes your hand,
counting the whorls on your fingers and thumbs,
hearing the clapper. You ask about essence,
you ask about time, you ask about questions.

The wind wipes the eyes. The bell goes
off, and on and on, and the flagstones shudder
with your approach. A small man auctions you.
He brings his gavel down, on the edge
of his polished pulpit. You are ready, smelted.

The bell goes off. It takes exactly three and
three-quarter minutes. Light carves a grin
on half-expectant faces, touches their tentative
fingers, the laundered linen. You have come
quickly back, as a new-laid, soft-boiled egg.

You have two coins

*You have two coins. Together they make 1s 6d. But one of the
coins is not a sixpence. What are the coins?*

- Reader's Digest Junior Treasury, 1960

You have two coins. They somersault
in your pocket, short trousers, khaki, your hand
trembling and twisting their silvered sweat.

They are loose changelings: they brain you,
like learning your grandad is dead
through a whispering door. Your mum

mentions the coffee in which he was
dipped when the night-nurses found him -
like the goldfish, resting on the level,

pellucid surface of the bowl: that clear globe
stripped of its continents. You scribble them
in your album: fish, grandfather, Himmler,

all on the other side. Puzzles and quizzles
and still you finger three weeks' worth
of sweets, which are hard-fast under your skin.

Flushed, alive, and five or six, you know nothing
but what you're not told. Your father roars,
Who poured away my gin? and, remembering

you helpfully emptied that crystal glass
of dead water, down the plug-hole, thinking how
its rivulets must be like the mincer's mince,

only faster, you mention it. Your father
roars again, the tears smarting his cheekbones.
He phones your best friend's dad, the one

who is and isn't an uncle. Laughs. Your mother
can't see the joke for the well-springs which
fill her eyes. She sips tea. And not coffee, and

your father, listening to *Two-Way Family
Favourites*, hears Peggy Lee. She's singing *Mr.
Wonderful*, and your mother requested it,

as amazing as the two coins, baffling your thumbs,
the ones that the truth is teasing you with:
except that she didn't, he made it up, he made it

all up, and she never explains it – never,
that is, until it is seventy-eight years later,
and she's ripping up a wad of odd snapshots.

A shilling and a sixpence. We only said that *one* of them was not
a sixpence.

Before Science

Before Science, there was the nature ramble,
the mould on milk, the inexplicable
pictures of mushrooms and smoke, the evaporation of breath,
words which coughed up freezing steam.
There was the big bang of the history teacher's car,
and rabbits with myxomatosis, and maybe polio, too,
and the strangeness of fathers (those who resembled
their sons. How?)

Before Science, there was 'Science'. It sat in a box
on the timetable, at the end of a Wednesday.
This was 'Science' before proper Science.
And it went like this:

you went to a room, a room filled with balsa,
and also knives. It was called 'The Balsa Room',
but on the door, it said 'Science'. You went in,
sat down, and you took the knives (sharper than glass),
and you cut the balsa
until you'd made a glider, which didn't fly.

On the stroke of four, the 'Science' teacher (before Science)
opened the cupboard, and drew out glue.
And he handed it round, until
you were stuck with it. Behind him, in the dark,
were two flagons, large ones, with lips
and proper stoppers. 'In here,' he said, as lightly as if
he had a balsa tongue, 'is Hydrochloric Acid.'
He paused.

'And this,' he paused again, 'is Sulphuric.' He spent
a long time over the syllables. They were pliable.
They were firm. They were
not like balsa. And so, in some dim, in some
indisputable way, we knew our era was up.
We painted our broken gliders, binned them,
and had our tea.

Sunday Afternoons

There was no sport on. Our fathers,
filled with gin, lay breathing

in the front-rooms; in the back,
our mothers fuddled over flowers,

or laid their prayer-books end to end.
They had no child but us.

We sat like national anthems,
pompous and circumstantial, hands

practising a saraband,
sinking like skiffs, or teasing sugar

over the silent fire. Clocks
held back, haughty or superstitious,

drolling their chimes behind shut doors.
In those days we had pantries,

sculleries, smoke-rooms,
cupboards under the front stairs.

There were no maids. We had
to ration our breath. Our houses

were fogged, were doldrums,
waiting for adolescence, for wars.

The Bridle Path

It was the walk we hated, waiting
in wellingtons and regulation sweaters, or, in winter,
belted into dark blue coats, like conscripts,
or trainee prisoners. Mud and frost
conspired underfoot. We marched in pairs
across its dirty demerara.

We perspired under aliases, or surnames:
first names were reserved
for frank chats with the vicar, after
infringing the hymnal, or drawing
cartoons on letters home.

And two by two, like parodies
of Start-Rite children, we went west, our ringworm caps
clenched to our heads:
down wild, dark aisles, beating the bounds,
the bounds we were out of,
past sheep who stood, gawping, where the pews
should have been.

The *bridle path*: we never saw
a single horse, or heard
the jangle of reins, the rub of a jodhpur, the hint
of a whinny. And so on. We didn't even
know it had anything to do
with horses at all. Hand in hand,
we did wonder, though, about weddings.

Pasts

The riveter, the joiner and the welder
pat my cropped head

as I wander, hand-held, under the ship
sitting on giant chocks.

They know who I am
better than I do: they smile to watch me travel

into the manager's office,
where I swivel on a leather seat.

One day all of this
will not be mine: I will make my way

along the wrecked remains of the yard,
no longer astonished.

This is where I wasn't:
and nor were you. All I can do

is to slip you into the history, second-hand.
Talking to me, you touch the pulse

of who you are, of places
where I never went. Somehow they collide.

The chauffeur, the plater, the paint-shop hooligans
show you the hull, the buckled deck,

and call you by your name.
They recognise you. They look unsurprised.

Boarding

You were the *head boy*, you said. You might
      have said it twice, I don't know,
I was too busy watching the comedy of scorn
      creasing your lips.

In your case, you hung from the parapets at night
      reading Kierkegaard naked
except for a pair of non-matching hockey socks
      and smoking a Turkish spliff.

This was after you had run back, in disguise,
      from mixing it with gypsies
who'd nicked some bottles of Bollinger
      from the local baroness.

Ah yes, I said: but that was only because
      in my school you were made head boy
because you were immensely *clever*.
      You raised your eyes like drawbridges.

Maybe that wasn't such a
      clever thing to say. In fact, it was
pathetic, as in fallacy, and there was
      a storm, instant, like the start of friendship.

Take Your

punishment like a man, suggested my father.
His hand was as flat as a platitude:

I ran over and round the bed,
more athletic than Bruce Tulloch, Abebe Bikila

and Fanny Blankers-Koen. It was the first time
he'd seen me sprinting. It gave him pause.

I had packed the bed with soap,
with shampoo, with Medicated Izal, with Vim:

better than teddy bears, I figured.
He held his breath in his hands, offended

by my Olympian feat. It was thirty years
before he snapped his arm

in the process of dying. He took his chance,
and hit me till the tears

welled like silver medals in my eyes.
You have, he said, to play by the rules.

Somewhere he saw me, misty-eyed,
finally breasting the tape.

Mirror Images

My grandmother is five. It is the final
year of the nineteenth century.

There is a banana on her mother's dressing table,
which she eats (the banana that is).

Caught with a smear on her lips
and the flopskin of the banana, she says

'It was not me who ate it.
It was the little girl in the mirror.'

You come to me in the twenty-first century and tell me we are
mirrors. I am my grandmother, and yours as well. Here is the
dressing table. I see you in her furs, with her chauffeur, calling
me *ducky*. Her, not the chauffeur. I'm five.

There is no banana.
You ate it.

Shoplifting

It began with the perfume counter
There were too many boxes and too many bottles
The scent went for his gullet
He was holding a fan of fivers
Their voices were soft and smooth and lipstick
They asked him if he was being served
They asked him if he was after anything in particular
Someone sprayed incense on the heel of their hand
He gagged himself with his scarf
His heart began to choke like a motor
They talked to him in apostrophe
He wafted his right arm
Sweat began drooling his backbone
He became unconscious of other customers
He lay down like a queue
They carried him into a porcelain backroom
Someone rinsed out his mouth with rosewater
Another one broke his clothes open with pincers
They had no local anaesthetic so they used foreign
He came to in a coma
They were speaking to him like children
They found the stopped watch in his pocket
He never paid for it
They fitted it to his wrist like mechanics
When he woke up he was gone

Rooks

You were there, then,
when the rooks took each
other off, with their blimey flight,
and their pantaloon thighs.

You heard. They dorked and yawned
in the silhouetted trees,
and their medley of nests
wedged
like toughened tonsures they'd
nicked from mad monks.

They croaked like parody frogs,
like diesel engines crossed
with a Johnny Cash tribute band, in Shanghai.

You said *rooks* without looking,
and whirled me round.
Thin air. And in it, the rooks paired
and partied, and flew
endlessly round, out of reach, their
motors going, light-headed, in berk circles.

After Auden's *Musée Des Beaux Arts*

About celebrity, they are always right,
The Young Pundits: how well they televise
Its shallow ambition; how it works best
When someone vain is pouting or trying the tango or just
                                    feeling a spider bite;
How when some viewers are eagerly, desperately hoping
For a classic serial, there always must be
Others who do not actually want to watch one, groping
For a zapper down the sofa's sides:
They calmly insist
That even a great adaptation can be safely stored
On some other channel, while a Z-list
Of celebs gets on with their nebulous lives and a fraudulent
                                    horde
Pimps up their indolent careers for a fee.
Take Channel 4's *Big Brother*, for instance, how everyone turns
                                    quite
Happily over from drama; the viewers might
Have cheered the actors, the sheer suspense,
But for them it is not a particular issue; it may gleam
As it must do on the other side, with elegantly designed
Costumes; and the expensive sensitive script that some might
                                    find
Simply amazing, a joy thrilling, even intense,
Is something to dump while Chantelle lives the dream.

Quiz Contestant Blues

after Auden

Over the ether my image flows,
I'm the weakest link on the trivia shows.
My brain is rattling but I must reply,
I'm a quiz contestant, I don't know why.
The host rakes over my life with cheek,
My wife's in the audience; her smile is weak.
Tarrant has a hangdog, poker face,
I can't answer his questions, I'm in disgrace.
Noel knows his numbers, I don't know any;
I might win a quarter-mill, might win a penny.
I gave them a ring, and they put me through;
I want the cash, but I haven't a clue.
The audience titter, and the audience squeal,
Ask me the question, Noel. Deal? No deal.
When I'm a veteran, I won't be restful:
All calls are charged, but not all are successful.

Life

There are those who argue that… because the rich man gets ice
in the summer and the poor man gets it in the winter things are
breaking even for both. Maybe so, but I'll swear I can't see it
that way.

— Bat Masterson, last words found in his typewriter, 1921

Wallop. And the spring goes in your step.
Dusk splits its sides like frosted glass. Beneath
a hammer-tested face, you crack a grin,
and hold it, mesmerised, between your teeth.

The first words which you ever hear: *Watch out!*
as you smell the axes hit the tempered timber,
exacting their revenge. A shattered beam
comes down, and leaves some spells inside your fingers.

If it ain't fixed, you've broke it. That's the motto.
Words aren't the last to go; they sit, impatient,
on paper, whilst you cut a final figure,
a shadow of a sprawl. The conversation

ticks in your trap, and peters out. There's some
who'd call this spasm merely maladjusted.
I say: you step on ice, it always fractures.
You beat your heart until the thing is busted.

The gunsmith types, and hears the last report
unfinished, misses its echo. *Maybe so,*
but I swear I can't see it that way. Life's cut short,
while a weather-beaten moon swings to and fro.

Selling up

The car heads home, driven by instinct,
not for the last time, but not too long to go:
the unlevel level crossing rumbles the wheels,
the signal box already in the hands of unlovely receivers,
and horses which have been pasted
        flat against that landscape
        already receding
into one dimension, after fifty years of standing
by the same unbroken broken fence.

Along the horizon, the water-tower and the mill,
the one no longer pumping, and the other flailing
        no sails at all,
        same as ever,
bleed into evening, begin the short trick
of vanishing entirely,
of swallowing themselves.
        The little hiccup of hill.
        The busted post-box.
All of this dissipates, like fug.

It might be that years later your children come
as you might do yourself and say
        This is where he lived.
The half-thought almost fools the sooty eye
but even as it strains to fix the view
the view itself resolves, dissolves,
the keys itch in the hand.
        This is what he called home.
        He must have seen it something like this.

Roadside

You fade into my shoulder like a fetch,
        an alter ego, a shade,
a sketch of myself, an outline, an etch
        as if you were made
out of the light in which we caught
        each other's image in a gasp,
out of smoke, resting in a delinquent port
        where the rowboats rasp
against the lip of the pier. You lean
        almost invisibly beside me
sharing the act, sharing the scene
        in which we confide we
were scooped from the same earth.
        Your mouth is cracked
as mine is. We are double-birth
        in fiction, in fact:
faces blotched and blurred
        by the dream we are sharing
like one paragraph, sentence, word,
        unstinting, flinted, unsparing.

Levels

Water is never level.

There used to be a level below this floor
but since they re-numbered them all
it's above and beyond us. A floor is not
a level here. It is a floor. The door to your right
opens on to another level entirely.

This is deep. This is too deep. This is
a five-pipe problem. This is a narrative
on several levels, all of them susceptible
to the keen interpreter of meaning.

Let me level with you: I love you
like tobacco loves a good grampus.

Slander

She accused him of being faithful.
'That's slander,' he said,
with his dove eyes and his malleable lips.
She lifted a laundry marker
out of her overalls, and scrawled it along
the ledge of his left hand.
'It's libel,' she said, 'and now it's
also indelible.' He took
his hand, scratched it with his tongue,
until the outline of ink
smirched itself, very faintly, behind his teeth.
Which he latched.
She left him that week. With his truths
paining his taste buds. She took her spanners,
her children, her hurt, her anger,
and lay under
greasy axles with other liars,
whose virtues she found it easier
not to believe.

Five minutes later

Five minutes later, bating his breath,
he came back through the front door,
to steal the clocks, and, by accident,
a barometer. They put up no resistance,
their hands still shifting slightly,
the cogs like silent abdabs, turning.

The grandfather took some doing:
taking it to pieces used precious seconds.
And then there were all the keys –
he had to tape them to the cases,
so that he didn't wind up with chaos.
It took patience, and effort, and sweat.

The next year he spent in purdah,
as if he were underwater, or deaf.
The counsel he kept was his own:
baffled, celibate, unfixing his life
from the mechanism of wife or family,
like taking apart a sonata.

Ten

– the age at which we meet,
pushed together like awkward furniture:

this is and *this is* and *why don't you*
and we sulk, a little, although

you're drawn to the red encyclopedia
I'm lugging under one arm, and

I'm taken by the cuts on your knees.
Even then you are the reckless one,

the tree-house genius. 'Do you know,'
you say, *'The Ancient Mariner*? I do'

and after that, it's plain sailing
through the ice floes and wild water

of words. Once you've unsprung
the lock on my tongue (two seconds)

we're running through farms and yards
at high speed, opening imaginary doors

and striking striking poses on outcrops
while weaving our hair into knots

(not that they weren't knots and tufts
before we set out on our adventure).

Look, say our mothers, they're playing
so *nicely*. But little do they know.

*

In Ruritanian rooms
we lean along the worn window-seats

fencing each other gently
with spirited and superior quotations

in imaginary Sanskrit.
The hearth is burning: we take turns

banking the blaze up with logs and logbooks.
Your hand beneath your chin

you ask me, 'How long will it be
until we go completely mad, seriously

mad as hatstands, as bandboxes, as castanets,
as crazy as the patina on antique billiard balls?'

We even know, at ten, that we're experts,
experts in the art of cracking up –

think Kerouac, think Zelda – why and where
we'll come unstuck, resisting the blizzards

which close in like unkempt strangers.
We dance across a polished parquet floor:

you say we have two right feet.
We take polaroids of the windows, which are

thickening with moorland snow.
I braid your hair, very slowly.

*

In a loft of forgotten apples and lost candles
and locked trunks full of unfamiliar letters

we give the known world the slip,
play truant, hide in a priesthole, whispering

or reading each other the best heresies
in an anthology of unforgiven sins.

We hang from ladders like bats.
We pretend to be orphans, abandoned

by frock-coated ruffians. We reach out
our ectoplastic fingers to read

thought as phrenology. The shadows bleed
our figures together, until we converge

one into another, laughing in tongues,
sometimes speechless, unselving in darkness:

solving each other like riddle-me-rees,
parsing each other like whimsical cryptograms.

Ante-rooms, parlours, sculleries, larders:
we chase the conversation through half-light,

scarpering across Persian rugs and rarefied carpets
in a world of satsuma, imari, forgotten porcelain,

peddling impressions, pulling improbable faces,
planning (of course) a succession of stunts.

*

A copper beech: its branches loiter
over the kitchen-garden wall. In the glasshouse

loaded grapes are pulsing with communion wine,
their juice as blue as barn swallows' wings:

our lips are soon rueful, suffused, our cheeks
streaked with the pulp. That evening we sleep

together, curled up in a forest of fleece.
Nobody finds us. Nobody looks. Nobody cares.

They think we are pillows, wedged in beds:
and they cannot hear the riot at dawn

as we wake in each other's dreams, talking
ninety-nine thousand to the dozen. For this

is what we were, when we were ten, when we
were poetasters and imps and wind-chimes

locked in the pure, the perverse logic of paradox,
wild elder children who believed in saints,

in the harmony of lanterns, in the martyrdom
of childhood, in the lovely litanies of birdsong,

before there were brambles, before there were thorns,
sworn into friendship, fragile as psalters,

held in a perfect parenthesis of now, before then,
when we were ten, ten years old, when we were ten.

A Modern Cautionary Tale

after Hilaire Belloc

The Chief Defect of Rose Elaine
Was using her capacious Brain
To type (for she eschewed the Pen)
To sundry Friends on MSN,
Espousing thus with horrid glee
Unorthodox Orthography –
In this, despite her Teachers' scorn,
She never ceased from Dusk to Dawn.
One night, she surfed the In-Between
Beyond her blue Computer Screen,
And vanished without trail or trace
Into the depths of Cyberspace.
Her Parents, who were unaware,
Discovering her Room was bare,
Shut down the System, learning later
That they could not retrieve her Data.

Bookworm

You lend me a book called *Obsessive Love*.
After a few hours I have fallen for it.
I wake in the night, read pages and pages.
I order it on Kindle.
I take it round to other readers, and leave it on their doorsteps
        at four in the morning.
I tape myself reading it.
I can't think of anything but the book *Obsessive Love*:
        even though it doesn't respond to me.
I build a shed in the yard out of extra copies.
I give it dog-ears and dirty thumb-prints.
I buy highlighters and annotate it.
I fill it with Post-Its.
I wake at night to make sure it is by my bedside.
I dream of running away with it to a library
        where there is nothing else on the shelves.
I spread it with peanut butter and eat it slowly.
I write it out in longhand, and shorthand.
I make a hat out of it.
I make another hat out of it.
I fill in the *o*s in *Obsessive Love*.
I am obsessed with *Obsessive Love*.
I can't read *Wuthering Heights* any more, because it isn't
        obsessive enough.
Nelly, I am *Obsessive Love*.
I fly to America and bang its author over the head.
Why should she take all the credit, she only wrote it.
It is my book now.
I composed it.
I have changed my name by deed poll.
You can call me Ob.
I won't answer to anything else.
You can't have it back.

Moment

Nothing headlong: just the hush
        of evening, the slow road-rush, sodium lamp-light,
as passing and pausing
        in the inner lane, you intertwine
your fingers in mine
        and they move in unison, like tendrils,
like children on swings, like things forgotten
        and gently remembered:

your face a keepsake, something I've come across
        in an album, a leaf pressed fresh,
our hands moving quietly
        through each other's hair, as if we were
testing some harpstrings,
        our mouths like unfamiliar language
heard in our wombs
        in the daze of the darkness.

You open the pages of my head
        and read me their words,
calm, but in earnest: and I fold them over
        and hold them, and speak to you:
and these are neither conversations nor
        catechisms, these are true, are
unrehearsed, and my almost-echoes
        spontaneous as spring rain.

Because they cannot be lost,
        because they are what we say
incapable of tears, because we need not fear
        that we will shiver or break,
and because they are answers
        to questions we never asked,
but spoke them together
        without a shiver, our two truths,

neither jealous nor knowing ever
        what our futures contain,
this was a perfect moment,
        a blessing, a pact, a refrain.

Keyboard

You lost a letter
on your keyboard and you send me
posh participles
from your palpitatin fin ers
as if you had joined
the red-faced sorority
of the local hunt
and hammered your thou hts
with ribald lee
after stridin over the dales
your thi hs naked, ales sweepin
the landscape
and found me in the lon rass
waitin for you like a randee
where the quick brown fox
jumped over the lazy do
hopin you'll reet me
and rant me
and o with me
yes and o with me
and rip my body once more

40

Dead Weight

And of course what gives the risk its edge
is the indistinct possibility
that while we are raiding each other
like larder thieves
in search of the perfect meal
that one of us (me, you suspect)
will come to a sudden end
and keel into your opening and closing arms.

Thoughtless of me, it would be,
but despite the privacy of love, you might have to
call an emergency friend
who'd give you strength
to fold me into my clothes
after lugging me to the shower
washing me tenderly (but speedily)
and towelling me within an inch of my death.

Perhaps as you tipped me
into the boot of your car, you'd see me
smiling up at you, eyes like milk,
my last words still inked
on chalk-white lips. And out of breath –
like me, it goes without saying –
you'd touch my forehead once or twice
and whisper what used to be my name.

Driving Away

You stepped out into the snow, slowly, and I drove away.
In the faff of traffic, I turned
and ran my hand
over the passenger seat. Usually, you leave, as you know,
something behind: wallet, glasses, nail polish, phone,
your tickets, fragments of sleep.

There was something you'd said.
I held your voice up to my ear, composing replies.
Tell me when you are home and safe: I ran your message
gently, pressing the pedal, sensing
how your absence is always present, how I find you moving
through these familiar streets.

Causeway

This is no land for a bridge:
arches aren't needed, their inverted curves

as useless as euphoniums
in a string quartet. The dunes

will do, their rough unsteady pasture
perfect for opening

the way to the island.
Over the pubic bone of sand

where the careful traveller
watches the waves

startling apart, and soothing
to stillness, we may

lay the low road, we may raise
a half-day causeway,

one that's prepared to wait
for the water's tongues

to swallow each other,
to meet when it's needed.

*

Tonight it is closed,
this half-lost crossing

from shore to shore
and the sea weeps

about my ankles, my shins:
watching the currents

rankle and close their long lips
like a healing scar

until the pale road over
the shale-grey sea

is hidden and shriven
by the riding waters

while I rock helplessly
in the nearby inn

biding the hours away
and watching the island lights

empty themselves
across the reach of the swell.

*

At dawn, I gaze at you
phrasing your eyes

so that they sift the syllables
on my silted tongue

and walk with you gently
down to the muddy track

that appears between the
curtains of water, receding,

and I think I am dead
except that you loosen your hair

and stretch yourself out
beside me, facing me,

both of us held in a transient
instant of love,

slippery, illuminated
by the sweltering moon

creating a causeway
over the softening mattress

of cobbled sand and breathing
undrowning

in the silken shallows
from here and to there.

Girders

I tuck my Mazda in behind the lorry. It's loaded
with long green girders and, gazing at each H,
I imagine a fatality: mine,

a girder irking itself over the edge, and yerking
itself through my head. I hardly hear
the windscreen go; and I don't feel

my head hurtling backwards, its thoughts,
its constant script, its images of you,
coming to rest in the back-seat tip:

boxes and a scram of paper, the usual smatter
of leaky pens and coins, the residue of receipts.
I shrug that off. The lorry is waiting

to turn into restless traffic. It will take
a long time to shift. Bored, I sidle to its left,
thinking to tack into its slipstream

whenever the moment comes. It could be ages.
But it arrives, that gap, and I run in parallel
as it grinds to the far lane, turning right.

I touch the pedal, let the lorry steam away
into its groove, leaving me in its wake. And so I'm
thirty feet adrift when the girder

topples towards me, mid-air, in a vague
but helpless trajectory. The braking's quick:
an instinct that brings me quaking to a halt,

six inches from the metal. The van behind me
shunts to a standstill. The lorry-driver lopes
out of his cab, makes vague and helpless signals.

I stand by the car, dreamless. It's missed me.
My idle loop to the left has drawn me away
seconds from death. I think how you kissed me

with silent abandon, only two hours earlier,
the way our bodies vamped and shifted
through the gears, the way your blue eyes

blew their fuse, and I wanted to tell you,
look, I am alive, I love your sure-sweet tears
as we drive this highway together.

Blend

Under an arch, under a bridge perhaps,
we cadge each other's language:

in the dark, drawling our childhoods,
we find ourselves unshuttered, wake our eyes

beneath identical lids. The towpath runs
along the mirroring water, and we place

our worn boots into the same soft mud,
remembering the nights when voices

scratched at our heads, and told us both
that we were made of harm, and that our thoughts

were dangerous, that we were sure
to be tarnished, that we would never fit

into the world of virtue. They unseamed us
with threats and terrors, insisted we were

different, different, different. Now we stand
like vandals, cut from the same leather,

exchanging accusations, recalling mornings
when we were made to stand, on the ledge,

to understand our sins. I screamed and threw
the kitchen knives into the air; you stood

and held the heated air in your shut lungs.
Our heads were arcing and sparking

with suppressed energy. We were the wild.
We were the bad example, the eldest child.

Here in this damp air, breathing this fug,
somehow survivors, our thoughts are lamplight

burning from the same strange source.
The water's images reveal us; we look down

and see our shadows mingle. It is no wonder,
although it is wonder too, that when we turn,

we crush our mouths together, move our hands
in slow adagios, inhabit one another, speak

in unpicked riddles, drawn by the morning
breaking over the city. And far from pitiless,

we strip each other to the hidden skin
and huddle up, tender and incensed, make

love like laughter, taking each other together
against the wall, born in the same caul,

not like strangers, but like one perfect cry,
always giving, always moving closer,

our eyes blending, unendingly as one,
and different from others, as they told us,

in a world, in a space, holding ourselves,
opening and closing like sea-anemones.

Weave

I hold my breath until my tongue's in tatters,
and my lungs, arrested, pause inside my chest.
We had a great day: everything that matters
flowed between us, and never came to rest –
when we are in our spate, when clauses close
and open, when we play with punctuation,
the streets fade out, the sound of traffic goes
into the ether. It is a strange sensation
to hear our voices lift and lilt and shift:
to see them spiral, sense that they're in tune,
catching the wave, catching each other's drift,
and never to falter through the afternoon.

I sit inside your car, which could be mine:
chaos of paper, particles of dust
and bits of clothing, thrown with no design,
like all the meanings still to be discussed
between us both. Our road-map's not been spread,
our route unknown, because of missing pages.
And once, you cannot turn, you hold your head
face forward, eyes rimmed red. Feels like ages
until you grab composure, but it's quick:
I sit politely by you, till you settle.
I feel I know what makes your senses tick,
that we were hammered from one sheet of metal.

The church is cool, the psalters neat and worn;
it tugs quotations from us (yours correct!),
and we explore it, almost like we're drawn
towards the stone, to inch about, inspect
the lottery of life, the faded carving
of names and numbers, while the bell, unchiming
hides behind glass. We are a whole, unhalving
and halving again. Of course, it is bad timing:
strolling like this reminds of the random
nature of things. And we weave through the town,
grasping this nettle, friends in endless tandem.
You throw me words, your window half-wound-down.

Going Dutch

Let's split our difference, I said,
we're both broke. You took my fingers
out of your pocket,
clutching a handful of coins.

You saw the first half of the film;
I saw the second. Afterwards,
we ran to a restaurant, where I ate the main meal,
and you the starter and the

sweet thing about it was the way
there was no need to talk.
Both of us kept our own counsel,
both of us were shut up

in the same conversation.
We couldn't face each other
except in the shop window
where you browsed

the clocks, and I thought of the time
when we would spend
the whole of our bank account together.
And we would divide

the days and nights,
sleeping in separate dreams, having a funny
turn, and being conscious
or unconscious. A double act:

your punch-line, my joke,
the solo cigarette we lit and stubbed,
all one of us, and so,
your place or mine?

Illegal

I'm driving through a froth of rain
windscreen wipers prising away the night
in an onrush of cars, lorries,
the coastal road rolling ahead of me, a silent frenzy
of leaving and arriving, and

shifting from lane to lane, my eyes
pressed against the view, when you
text me, and I fumble for the phone, and open your
message like motorway madness.
Take care, you say, don't read these words,

safe journey.

Whitemail

Unless you don't return the letters that you've
not yet sent me, proposing
a scandal-free weekend in somewhere nowhere near
Bournemouth or Bognor,
then I'll certainly have to refrain –
from telling your wives and other unloved ones
about how you never led me on,
about the promises of hot nights you kept
not offering, the way you never said you
seduced me, because you didn't –
how could you
when you've never even seen my packet of snaps,
my albums, the rose-tinted postcards
I might have had saved, had you the foggiest
how much I love your
absence from all corners of my life.
I enclose some money.
Spend it at leisure. Tell everyone
what you've not done.
Show them how dangerous you're not.
Otherwise –

Amy, Amy

after William Blake

Amy, Amy, turning white
In the wynehouse of the night,
What the needle drave & drew
Thy sailor's Betty Boop tattoo?

In what mood & in what wise
Rose the wings beside thine eyes?
Why thy warpaint? Why thy stare?
How the bouffance of thine hair?

What the pow'r, & what the soul
Gave thy smoky voice controll?
Why the rehab? what the ache?
Where your husband (also Blake)?

When the Spice Girls hit the chart,
What the point? & where their art?
With what blues didst thou break free?
Who made them did not make thee.

Amy, Amy, turning white
In the wynehouse of the night,
What mere mortal anguish'd cry
Dare match thy fearful artistry?

At The Consulate

It is so difficult to hold a conversation
with a bird up your nostril –

cardinal or spoonbill, same difference,
it's hard to control your breathing

and to balance a champagne cocktail
at the same time, too.

The little diplomat, slicked hair,
with the wife made of white diamonds,

he found it very hard indeed
to be polite, and in seven languages,

with a nose full of tyrant,
no matter how perfect its peck.

Por favor, por favor, he cried out,
nasally, as well he might,

and the visiting ecumenical
took him into a deserted vestry

and tugged it out by the tail.
If you ask me, a good canapé

is worth the ambassador's drawl,
his bragging, his obsession with Verdi,

his splayed hands, his humdrum humming,
what with a redstart in his sinus –

but one must observe pleasantries
in case of a coup, in case of jeeps

and the closure of the only airport,
and the sound, over a tannoy,

of a rebel leader, still in fatigues,
with a manakin in his mouth.

Check Out

There was a problem with the tills; and so,
since we were adrift, and passionate, we stripped
off and lay, quite naked, between the two
dividers. The belt was still. We lay
in a loose clinch, our heads restful against a pound
of very new potatoes. Beneath us, the scratched
tongue of blackened rubber; above us,
striplights with flickering interest. We made love
with all our shopping. Other customers, their faces
pursed with impatience, looked across,
and noted our purchase, the two-for-ones, the brands
of bargain beans, the little luxuries of breath,
the loose sighs of our fruit, the middle class olives
just beside our tender, heated feet.
The manager was called, and flinched his key
in the lock, oblivious, over-riding the errors
of the assistant. And then, juddering, the belt began
its uncertain journey. By this time,
we were absorbed in a conversation of limbs,
fourth in the queue, and pomegranate-pink. We came
to, we came together, undid ourselves, our faces brazen
and glazed, were swiped, and slid
out of our selves, and into our (folded) clothes.
You packed, I paid, and our groceries
were bagged. You had to help me
with the chip and pin. Chewing her lips like soft gum,
the assistant switched to us, with a trainee smile.
'Do you,' she said, half-turning, and uncertain
which of us to ask, 'want any cashback?'

Supplements

Supplements are such a struggle:
Business, Media (full of air);
Leisure; Style – I couldn't care
two hoots. I watch the binmen juggle
gamely, lift my whole collection –
Property, Appointments, Culture,
and, off to meet the local mulcher,
'Recycling' (one-off, special section).

They lift, their muscles hardening,
Sport (with World Cup chart inside);
Education; TV Guide;
Family; Pensions; Gardening,
which leaves me with the News Review,
and also with the News itself.
I scan them, line the kitchen shelf –
no time to read the damn things through.

So there it goes: another tree.
I bought it for the DVD.

Inventions

He made them up from manuals of hands.
At first he was all
fingers and thumbs and thick lip,
tied knots in knots, that
sort of thing. All parcel fever.

The first batch was botched, they neither
wept nor slept. There was hiss
and boo all over the shop, the floor
was strewn with it, like an outbreak of petals.

Hydraulics: poor. He swore
at the instructions until they suppurated
under his beaded eye.
The strength returned. The crude oil
no longer curdled, the screws whirled,
there was a scream of pure steam.

By the ninth midnight, he was working
at full tilt, he was a scrantum of action,
the words whizzed past, the neighbours who complained
stayed to admire, and to make
great vats of sweet tea. The papers
were full of it, they beat the doors down
to feast their faces, the audience scored him,
his mother sent him a fiver.

And this is what he had made:
the story of a trout which had been tickled,
a handful of lavender,
and the way that strangers smile when they reach
the end of a road, and bless their homes.
He never looked back. From that moment,
he was made.

Sirens

Ooh-wah. Ooh-wah. Ooh-wah.
I wait in the offshore water, listening to sirens
on Friday nights. They pulp the air,
hunting the prom for prey, all feathers
and blinding blue. Sometimes two,
sometimes three, looking for raff, for scalps.

Ooh-wah. Ooh-wah.
It's safer underneath the pier, strapped up
against a strut. The sirens bat their wings,
patrol the coastal road, and draw
dangerous strangers aside,
drag them towards their doorways.

Ooh-wah. Ooh-wah. Ooh-wah.
The crowds are heaving. Wild, the sirens prowl,
bagging their victims, all alfalfa hair
and strip-lit eyes. They swallow up
everything that moves. I huddle here.
I mind my own beeswax.

Pink Mist

When I think of you I see you
wrapped in delicious fire   in ribbons
shot through with wild delight
a strange transparency of bone   skin   flesh

and when I lookthrough you
I feel your luscious heat
almost basting my face
can trace you   hmm   with my fingers

The song left your lips
like rose-hip halva   I heard the roar
and I exist   blood-kissed   and the world is true
when I am here pink-misting you

Pink-misting is US army slang for vaporising an enemy with a shell

When I think of you I see you
wrapped in delicious fire   in ribbons
shot through with wild delight
a strange transparency of bone   skin   flesh

and when I lookthrough you
I feel your luscious heat
almost basting my face
can trace you   hmm   with my fingers

The song left your lips
like rose-hip halva   I heard the roar
and I exist   blood-kissed   and the world is true
when I am here pink-misting you

Behaviour

'I am sure you did your best, my dear.' – Mrs. Gaskell, *Cranford*.

And one day she went to breakfast
and found she had odd feet:

one was cuffed, the other flared,
it could have been worse, it could have been

a whorl or a turnip.
'What the hell,' said the headmistress,

'are you up to? Yesterday you looked
presentable enough.'

'Yesterday,' she said,
'This was a boys' school,

and I came down in the wrong gender.
There was no fuss.'

She stood, slightly unsteadily,
pleased with this answer,

her smiles uncurling like tea-leaves.
That (of course) was uncalled-for,

so they rang for a fleet of matrons
who arrived in full formation,

wielding their teeth,
their eyes like ageing Strepsils.

The headmistress stroked her face.
'Cheek,' she said, absently,

and, under her clapboard tongue,
'Boys will be boys.'

X

marks the spot, presumably on maps,
although ten out of ten Romans might, perhaps,

disagree, in disgruntled Latin. It's what
my great-great-grandmothers carve, red-hot,

into the register, the first great marital kiss,
in trembling ink, in black, and in the bliss

of wondering which child might fill them,
only, in birth's great blood, to kill them.

It's the wrong answer, marked. It is pinned
to the heart of the deserter, with the wind

shivering his eye, while the squad, slo-mo,
take aim. It's the alternative brand to Omo,

the anonymous other, the invisible witness,
the chromosome we share. It confers fitness,

talent, the rich blister of instant fame.
It gives unknown planets a temporary name.

Algebra loves it, and provides it with curls.
It separates the boys from the girls,

is Christ incarnate, is the film with the cleaver,
incontinent language, and characters who heave a

sigh as they strip and peel, and ache and hunch
with lust. It marks the eye, when a sucker punch

lands on a cartoon cat. It is larger than large.
You vote with it. The knitter, Madame Defarge,

did not pronounce it, watching *les cheveux*
of the severed heads, sweating. Some prefer

to stick one on a family tree, instead of an *m*.
We scratch out a calendar with it, and condemn

days to oblivion's drivel, as months fly by:
thus we subtract, where others may multiply.

The descendant of slavery razes his name,
and uses the letter as proof. It's stamped with shame

on the forehead of the thief, now an amputee,
to distinguish him from the soldier. Out at sea,

it shows where a rock lies. It could be danger.
I am Mr. X. I am alien. I am stranger.

Stevie at the seaside: the true story

Actually, everyone heard him, the dead man,
But he wasn't worth saving:
He was proud of his prowess at sport
And not drowning but waving.

He wore tight trunks, and showing off his strokes
Like butterfly, Australian crawl —
He's out of his depth let's leave it that way,
Agreed all.

If you're sipping a cocktail at noon
On golden sands
And someone is boasting off the coast
Who needs a show of hands?

Oh, yes yes yes, it was deliciously warm
(Too hot for the attention he was craving)
He may sink I think the lifeguard said
When he starts drowning not waving.

From Wilfred Owen: *Festival*

... If you have sunk, with every mud-mad step,
Into a chasm carved out by the rains,
All senses dulled as ditch, putrescent slop
Feculent as a midden where there churns
Some smelted hell invented by strange demons...
If bells awake you, tolling in your ears,
Filling your blistered head with cursèd omens,
Omens which bring no sentience, nor pause...
If you have marched your feet through curdling slime,
To roar applause at brash, untuned guitars,
Their chords as heavy as the inland loam
'Neath calls unholy as unwholesome curs...
My friend, you would not treat a wide-eyed niece
To comic tales of opiates and slurry,
And tell the old lie, of eternal peace
At Glastonbury.

Biffo Days

an anagram of Invictus *by W. E. Henley (' I am the captain of my soul ...').*

Not, I cannot, cannot do a single thing;
I'm happy as can be.
The thought of heaven often makes men sing
My goodness! Lucky me!

The Lord protects me all the while.
Tho' He cuddles me if I doubt — and you.
Oft, He causes me to crow, chortle, titter, smile —
Do accept it: He is a wish come true.

How much we do both (both!) have fun (fun!)
After one (hard, hard, hard, hard) prays:
Not difficult, not to me: a v. fit, country ray of sun —
Hic, Lord, what biffo days!

Debt? Regrets? Had not, not a qualm:
It's been an utter ball.
My life has been a charm:
I'm powerless, after all.

Air Force

Oh you were perfect, a perfect
hurricane, they said. They had words for you, words
with you, a whole string of indignant nouns.

And all because of the day, windless and bright,
that they lined you up like a squadron
of roses and tulips, in bloom

for the photographer under his prayer-shawl,
flash-gun up like a ping-pong paddle
guiding in nervous flight crews.

Just before the powder blew
you mussed your hair up, because you could,
because you were born

with a rebel heart. Look at the picture. I do.
Under the prim and cloudless sky, of all the attentive faces,
I can only pinpoint one: yours.

Inkblots

'There was an inkblot test, and I mean the big deal for us was, don't see anything sexual or unusual or weirdo, just pick something you know. I said, 'Well it looks like a butterfly to me.' We didn't want to be perverts, you know.'

Astronaut Charles Duke
on the aptitude tests for lunar missions

Spread-eagled eyes, spring heels, and spaced-out hair.
Skinned bed, broken head, the bleeding obvious:
someone had flexed their muscles.
They lay like lumps of pumice.
There was pulp, but no fiction.
This guy says: 'You see what I see, Amos?'
I held my tongue. 'Well,' I said,
chewing the moment like a piece of pork,
'it looks like a butterfly to me.'

There was movement in the boulevard that night,
a surreptitious shift in the wind.
We heard them coming, out of the ozone,
with crickets under their lips, as if they only
spoke to strangers. There was dew on their foreheads,
mucus in their lids, the stink of dishrag.
They dragged their legs. It was unbelievable.
A woman, white-hot with laughter, and heavy with her hips,
came up to me, close. She said:
'You see what I see, Amos?' I took stock.
I stood as still as a cornered cockroach.
'Well,' I said, 'it looks like – '

'Now don't say the B word, Amos,' she said,
puckering her thumbs, and reaching under her wig.
'You seen a chrysalis? Ever?'
She had me there. She had me well and truly.
Her cheeks were scored,
striated like war-scarred Pawnee braves.
Even her irises were tattooed.
She showed me her shoulders, peeling back
the raincoat (it was a tough summer) and said:
'You see what I see you see, Amos?'
I mulched my lip, and she spread her sexy wings.
'Well,' I said, hesitant, 'you look like butter, you look like –'
'Yes?' 'All right,' I said, thinking of craters, of blue-bruised sky,
'You look like the stars and stripes.'

Hound Dog by Robert Herrick

Julia, should'st thou wawl and bay,
Throughout the night as through the day,
Thy huckleberry tears resound,
That some, I fear, think thee a hound.
But when I gaze into thy face,
No yearning have I for the chase:
Has thou a coney ever caught?
Doubt this, our amity is naught.
Permit me, too, to question thee
Upon thy sworn nobility,
For all thou hast a silken breast,
There is no substance to thy crest.
A harrier thou seemest, sure,
But mongrel-eye'd, thy blood impure:
Thou ne'er hast pluck'd a buck or doe,
For which our concord may not grow.

Distinctive Mongolian Eyes

One of the reasons given for the mistaken shooting in a tube train of Brazilian Jean Charles de Menezes was apparently that he had 'distinctive Mongolian eyes'.

If you've nothing at all to declare
but are thinking of wearing disguise,
hire a beard, but better not wear
distinctive Mongolian eyes.

When you are leaving your flat
and you're tempted to cause a surprise,
swipe a strange hat, but leave it at that:
no distinctive Mongolian eyes.

Innocent though you may be,
here is a word to the wise:
dress up as a tree, but don't seem to see
through distinctive Mongolian eyes.

Distinctive Mongolian eyes
are a badge, like a burqa or kilt:
even if real, they are sure to give rise
to a sudden suspicion of guilt.

You may be whiter than white,
but this is what I would advise:
many take fright at even the sight
of distinctive Mongolian eyes.

Parking Problems

You enter the hospice by an automatic door,
clutching your hold-all, -all in this instance

being not much: slippers, night-dress, the pills
(which are not working), and the spare

glasses, change, books you will not read.
There is no screaming in the hospice corridors,

but somewhere there's a hum. The mattress breathes.
In every ward, a white-haired woman sleeps,

undressed to the nines, lifting suspicious lids
with more than effort. The art of conversation

has been cracked into backchat, turned into banter.
You're called by the wrong forename, draw

yourself into yourself, and faddle round
in the lucky dip which is your snap-shut handbag.

Every 'thank you' has an edge. And every night
you shrivel just a little. Now your teeth

don't seem to fit at all, rest in a plastic pot
which once held cole-slaw. Down the gangways

the guests and visitors come walking, to be shown
the coffee-cupboard, and the long thin handles

of the taps, like silver clavicles, or something
unspeakable from a surgeon's kit, although there aren't

surgeons in these soft-shod halls. On the way out –
the vague direction of everyone in sight –

you see the notice, stapled to the brick, above
the crooked line of cars. *Short Stay Only.*

Bedside

A time-and-motion man, I scrutinise
the ward in which my mother, still, will
finish her dying. It is full
                    of rectangles:

door, bed, bin, the silenced television,
pillow, window, the locked-up cupboard
of pills. And centre-stage
                    on a dais of light

what's left of her is shell, as silted air
shifts its way through parched and punished lips.
She knows, I think, I'm here,
                    or just about,

her syllables constricted. What we see:
how shallow all her breathing has become,
as if she hovered on the very edge
                    of her wake.

I hope you don't remember me like this:
said yesterday. I held her thinning fingers,
produced imperfect platitudes, that we'll
                    recall only

the person who's within her. Lies, wild lies:
what I will take away and to a grave
is this - this wretched, skeletal affair –
                    this parody

of being human. You cannot scrape this stuff
from the cracked enamel of memory,
from the surface of heart.
                    How gingerly

her eyes gasp open, pupils milked, the rims
as grey as sealskin, soft as abalone.
She stares at the air, attempts to swallow it,
                    three times,

and vanishes. It's stunning. They've told me
her hearing may hang on. So here I am, brimming
with whisper, soundlessly loud, out of this
                    broken mouth.

My mother is a field

abandoned by farmers, poor grazing perhaps,
even the air is fallow,

and its fences subside like parallelograms
taken from graph paper

and asked to support a heavy fog
which has been foisted on poor pasture,

besides which, the gates have been padlocked,
the milkman has never collected his churns

from the entrance, boulders have rolled in
and bedded themselves in the brush

where scutch and razor-wire weed have taken
the place of the clover, it is

all grown over with thorns, and nettles
have covered the face thereof, while ramblers

dismiss it as a prospect for picnics, and
someone has dumped some split sacks, spilling

caustic stuff which is already caked
across the brush, and as for reclamation, the council

believes that the property's private, meaning
that I'm the only one who knows

what all of this is, as I navigate my way, scrupulous,
testing my second-hand metal detector.

The Last Time I Paid For Your Dentures

you were already dead and had been
for four months and more.
And they didn't fit you either,
so you said, and the man who measured them
made less sense than you.
You were like that, always a smart remark
in your head, always a last retort.
Many's the time someone was given
the flash of your tongue: a nurse, say,
or a waitress, or anyone who did not know
the difference between a lip of a tea-cup
and the rim of a whisky glass.
All the same there are days when I wish
you'd press those burned lips
against my cheek and catch me out
in an ill-thought phrase,
some solecism, something we understood,
me and your big mouth.

Supermarket

The supermarket is packed with grief.
Every aisle is full of it: the shelves groan
with punnets of grief, with bargain
buckets of the stuff, with bits of it
covered in clingfilm. It comes in different
sizes, grief you can snack on, or grief
which is good for you, organic and barn-fed
and low calorie grief, grief you can
get your right eye teeth into, grief by the counter
in case you're tempted to add an extra
transaction of grief. But there is junk grief, too,
own-brand, cheap, five for the price of two,
microwaveable grief, grief for the whole family,
or grief of course for one.

You wander down a separate aisle and you
come to grief, grief with tickets tacked over tickets,
grief at the end of its shelf-life, grief
with one or two days or hours to go,
weeping slightly, sweating under the lights,
raw grief, chilled grief, grief which has been
boned and cured, grief by the slice, or
grief you can guarantee will make you hurt
or your money back. Some of the grief,
even the fresh grief, has been flown in
from whole countries of desperation,
from grieving and unlit destinations. You ask
for the latest grief, and they take you
to snazzy brands, exotic grief you've never
so much as imagined. You fill the trolleys
with loads of grief, until the tannoy tells you
that you have five minutes left to check it out
at the counter. Do you want any help
unpacking this grief, says the girl with her name
stapled sadly to her heaving chest, as she
swipes the grief slowly.

You meet me in the car park with your grief.
You have more of it than me. Look at my
grief, I say, and feel guilty. Your grief is far more
shocking than mine. You look across, holding
several till-rolls which itemise so many kinds
of grief. I offer to push your grief to the car.
No emotions, no feelings, you say. I wish I could
give you the grief that you give to me, you add,
and you thank me for helping you with your grief,
as you load it into the boot, and you stand away,
holding your grief together, while mine spills
all over the pale grey pavement. I'll always love
your grief, you tell me; it's much like mine is.
And now we must live with our grief laid out
on the table where we list which grief we will tackle
on a daily basis. I think of the days when we
pushed our grief together, and blew it all away.
It was so much better. The grief of it, I mean.

Speechless

1

Her breath was halting, as if someone
had tucked a bomb under her tongue
and told her they were hiding
over there, behind that bush, under the laburnum:

true or not, out of her larynx
came nothing but paralysed air, and granulated
chat. She might just as well have been
talking to a papal nuncio

about the cost of her shopping.
It made no sense. The words ledged themselves
on nearby shelves, biding their time
before getting together, once all that breath

had been swept up. I imagined fitting
the broken phonemes in her mouth,
and, sitting back, applauding myself
for the act, like a spectator on a terrace

thinking himself into the boots
of the boy, the gawky one, overpaid, the lad
who knocks a winner in, in the fifth
minute of extra time. Yes: that pleased.

2

The teacher always asks you to own up,
all of you. You in the plural.
Some of your names have been thrown up,
and you stand at the front, a mural
composed of frozen innocence, choking
on smirks, stifling your laughter.
Own up, own up. You must be joking.

You stare at the rafters,
dreaming of Clara Petacci, her dark skirt
tucked in her thighs, and upside down,
like a cut tongue, lynched and inert.
The teacher sees you, sees you frown,
red-ticks you as what she suspected.
After ten minutes, you're disconnected.

3

Lady Tufnell watches the television
with the sound turned down, from her double bed
in which the late Lord Tufnell once decided
to end it all. The butler comes and goes,
spooning the blueberry goo through
her long-agog mouth. His feet leave clean heels
in the carpet, made from the finest Drysdales.

All night, the screen flitters and scintillates,
and the figures palpitate their lips,
or mash them together. Their skirmishing recalls
Lord Tufnell's trips to the interior, where he found
inanimate land, and a beast with three hearts.
He shot them, using a silencer.
Whatever he did, it was clean and pure. Decent.

Using certain lip-reading techniques, Lady Tufnell
dissects the scran of the scripts, as enacted
throughout the early hours. It would appear
that the man is asking for volunteers, to save
heroines from extinction. She writes a cheque.
In fact, the face at which she's staring, so attentively,
is feeding out football scores. *Tranmere, 2 -*

4

Suppose you leave your wife and children
after an argument that has lasted several years,
after breaking stuff, punching holes
through lath and plaster, all frustration,
        no idea
why ever you came to this pass, this moment,

and suppose you gather a handful of clothes
from the washing machine, clean,
then what did you say? You cannot invent
words you cannot remember, which must
have burst open between you. You leave
        on tiptoe.

Any street would seem strange; but this one,
loping downhill from your home,
is odd, new, fresh – shy like a bruised tongue –
the sight of it pinches your lips.
You don't know what will happen.
        What consequence.
Your mouth boils dry.

5

If my father's face had had jam on it,
I should have licked it away.

But it's clean-cold, and I examine it,
and kiss it. I say

You poor old bugger. He merely gurns,
his teeth out. The shop-bell sings,

and I breathe the lilies and the ferns,
held in this cell.

6

The deaf aren't dumb. They talk in semaphore,
hands grunting, muscles taut
with the effort of our listening: we are wired into
their loud eyes. They hear how we stare,
not at their teeth and tongues, but at their hairlines,
feigning incompetence. They reach forward
and shut our shouts out, thinning our insolence.

7

The ninth time, they made Caryl Chessman wait
until the very last minute. The reprieve
was signed, and, sighing, the secretary dialled
a wrong number. By the time she'd hung up, tried again,
the cyanide pellet had dropped in the vat,
the vat with the acid. It dissolved.
The gas-chamber must have had an echo;
he must have heard that splash. As reporters sucked
pencil-stubs with their tongues, the phone began to jangle.
It sounded like glass beads being trampled,
like crystal smashing, like china icicles.
It's with me, persistent, a burr. The gas cost a dollar.
I read the report in the paper, aged seven.

8

Lovers have Miranda rights. They can refuse
        to answer questions, in case
the truth spills out one afternoon, like engine oil.
        They can hold their tongues
for years, defy gravity, and keep their diaries blank,
        erasing every date. They muss
the months with their fingers - for to be open, to tell
        the whole of it, that's hard,
as dangerous as letting daylight break open
        shutters, screens, blinds.

9

Will you be quiet? Will you be quiet?
Will you be quiet? Will you be quiet?
Will you be quiet? Will you be quiet?
Will you be quiet? Will you be quiet?
Will you be quiet? Will you be quiet?
Will you be quiet? Will you be quiet?
Will you be quiet? Will you be quiet?
It isn't a question, is it?

10

He could do it, one leg strapped behind his back,
(since that is where the teacher aimed the cane)
– mental arithmetic, and plenty of it, in the corner.

Occasionally she would lob some long division
towards him, ask him (say) to divide 13,268
by 53 or 54, and to write up the answer, in chalk,

on the whale-grey board on the wall. He kept his
tongue in his cheek: better that than the cheek he'd
wrung from his tongue – exactly what had pressed him

into the corner in the first place. The rest of them sat
like an alphabet, wordless, at their desks,
unable to do much but raise their chastened hands,

mouth the wrong answers. She'd even chalked a D
on the megaphone she'd perched, absurdly, on his head.

11

[	] while eating.	[	] in the ranks.
[	] in class.	[	] for the dead.
[	] in church.	[	] in banks.
[	] at the back.	[	] in bed.
[	] in a lift.	[	] for the news.
[	] in libraries.	[	] in court.
[	] underwater.	[	] in queues.
[	] on air.	[	] the thought.

12

This is completely out of order.
This can't be fixed. This is beyond the kerfuffle
of plumbers. The Yellow Pages can't help.

A low drone: the pillion passenger has fallen
off the back of a bike, and cracked her throat
on the kerb. She doesn't make any sense.

I lean forward to catch a glimpse
of the bubbles on her tongue. It doesn't help
that I am drunk, nor that I am fourteen,

out on my first bender. It's New Year, just,
it's one in the morning. We saw the Triumph
lurching along the pavement, turning the bend –

we must have missed it by five minutes.
The next day, the local paper plays her name
under a grainy picture. Gives her age.

After that, she vanishes under a scum
of images, goes deep, moves wearily away
beyond my brain, into the frozen albumen

of someone else's family. Perhaps siblings.
The other overcoat (in the road) was dead,
speechless, thrown away by the night-time.

Void

Bring me your emptiness. Inspect me.
Fill me with your stones.
Let them weigh down my flesh, my bones.
It is time to reject me.

Stop my mouth with silt.
When the waves roll over my vacant face
Let there be no trace.
You must feel no guilt.

I am ready to be a shell
On the skeleton of the shore.
I know what I am destined for
Under the swell.

Roll my marbled eye
In its broken socket.
Here is my door. Lock it.
See me as blanked-out sky.

Lower my sails.
Leave me to sleep, to rust.
You must, you must, you must.
Think of me as nails.

I know you did not mean it.
Let me be mouthless, let me be moss.
When my body is full of loss
Do not attempt to clean it.

some text missing

but then we hardly need the words
that fill the void
                    inking as one
along the dotted lines
            spaces where we see

Your day my day
            such a thing and the

prinks and stalls.   all hesitation
but of course

            separation of this and this

Whole days are drowned. The weathercocks
spin on our steeples

            arts of the reservoir

Your skiff skids over the water
            towards what port
                        not know but when the storm
blows o

            and maybe we'll be free to say we

erase the pain
            you say sometimes   wonder
who know

and after all

            in sync. I know

Ringers

for Morgaine

– not as in *bells,* or *dead.* You come to my head
like an answer to any question
I've ever asked, and steam me open
with the heating words we've
found in our mouths:

if they laid us on shattered slats of ice
if we were slum-eyed fish set down together
on a market stall, pouting and touting
for passing custom
they'd see how similar our difference:

we're caught together by the camera
in a sham of silence
swimming through the rigmarole
beyond the sea, the nets, the hands, the knives
that mistook us:

even here, gasping for a fag-break,
stunning and silver like hotel cutlery
we're one and the same:
look beneath these scales, and hear our hearts
compounding.